Carl SAGAN

Ask courageous questions.

Do not be satisfied with superficial answers.

Be open to wonder and at the same time subject all claims to knowledge, without exception, to intense skeptical scrutiny.

Be aware of human fallibility.

Cherish your species and your planet.

—*Carl Sagan*

**Biography**

**Carl SAGAN**

Ellen R. Butts and Joyce R. Schwartz

*Lerner Publications Company*
*Minneapolis*

*To my sons, Daniel and Derek—intrepid explorers of
wondrous new worlds—for their constructive criticism
and enthusiastic support.*     —ERB

*To my father, Wallace Rubin, whose love of science
inspired my own.*     —JRS

**A&E** and **BIOGRAPHY** are trademarks of the A&E Television Networks,
registered in the United States and other countries.

Some of the people profiled in this series have also been featured in
A&E's acclaimed BIOGRAPHY series, which is available on videocassette
from A&E Home Video. Call 1-800-423-1212 to order.

Lerner Publications Company
A division of Lerner Publishing Group
241 First Avenue North
Minneapolis, MN 55401 U.S.A.

Website address: www.lernerbooks.com


Library of Congress Cataloging-in-Publication Data

Butts, Ellen.
    Carl Sagan / by Ellen R. Butts and Joyce R. Schwartz.
      p.   cm. — (A&E biography)
    Includes bibliographical references and index.
    Summary: A biography of a celebrity scientist who brought astronomy
to books, magazines, and television, as well as to his Cornell University
classroom.
    ISBN 0-8225-4986-7 (lib. bdg. : alk. paper)
    1. Sagan, Carl, 1934–1996—Juvenile literature. 2. Astronomers—
United States—Biography—Juvenile literature. [1. Sagan, Carl,
1934–1996. 2. Astronomers.] I. Schwartz, Joyce R. II. Title.
III. Series.
QB36.S15B88 2001
520'.92—dc21
[B]                                   99-35583

Manufactured in the United States of America
1  2  3  4  5  6  –  JR  –  06  05  04  03  02  01

# CONTENTS

*The Milky Way Galaxy includes the Sun, Earth, and the rest of our Solar System.*

# INTRODUCTION

**A**N ALIEN SPACECRAFT ORBITS HIGH ABOVE THE RED planet. Suddenly, a dome-shaped form breaks away and plummets toward the crater-scarred surface. It rushes down into the atmosphere. A shell pops off and a white parachute billows out, slowing the craft's descent. Three spidery legs, each with a flat disc attached, slowly unfold. The parachute falls away, and fire shoots out from beneath the craft. The strange lander slowly settles down. Dull gray in color, covered with odd bumps, it squats like a giant robotic insect on the planet's dusty surface.

An antenna pops out of its body and swivels skyward. A box on a short arm shoots out from one side. A collector at the end of a longer arm extends in front. Two eyelike cameras begin taking pictures. It is July 20, 1976. Earth has invaded Mars!

———————————

A crowd of scientists waits in the control room of the Jet Propulsion Laboratory (JPL) in Pasadena, California. Tension builds as they stare at the banks of computer monitors that dominate the room, waiting for the blank screens to blink to life. Will the lander touch down on firm ground or disappear into a dust-filled sinkhole? Will its cameras work? Will it transmit photos from Mars's surface to the orbiter? Will the orbiter relay the photos to Earth? Can this

7

mission succeed when so many others have failed? If it does, *Viking 1* will make history. It will be the first spacecraft to touch down safely and transmit clear, detailed photos from the red planet.

Carl Sagan waits with other members of the imaging team that will study the photos. He is a professor of astronomy and, at age 41, a well-known author, lecturer, and television personality. For more than thirty years, he has looked forward to this day. As a boy, he had been spellbound by science fiction stories set on Mars, losing himself in "a world of ruined cities, planet-girdling canals, immense pumping stations. . . . The people were red, green, black, yellow, or white and some of them had removable heads." Carl tried to imagine himself transported to Mars. He longed to explore its mysteries. But, as he got older, he realized that science fiction could neither teach him the facts about Mars nor show him how to get there. Only science could.

Carl and his fellow scientists wait as the time slowly passes. They will soon know if the mission is a success. So far, all has gone as planned. Eleven months earlier, the launch from Cape Canaveral, Florida, had been flawless. After ten months of space travel, *Viking 1,* consisting of an orbiter and a lander, had gone into orbit around Mars. The orbiter began sending back long-range photos of such excellent quality that the project team was able to use them to select a safe landing site.

Now the final phase is about to begin. Everything depends on the little *Viking* lander. It must separate from the orbiter and make a perilous three-and-a-half-hour trip. Traveling at more than 10,000 miles per hour, it will enter the Martian atmosphere. The angle of descent must be just right or the lander will burn up. As it nears the ground, its parachute must unfurl at just the right moment and its three small retrorockets must fire on cue or it will crash. If the lander reaches the surface safely, its cameras and instruments must work properly. Then, if all goes as planned, the first computerized images of the Martian surface will travel the 35,000,000 miles back to Earth. Transmission will take twenty minutes.

The wait seems endless. Then, as the *Viking* team watches in awe, an image begins to form on the monitor screens—the first distinct picture ever relayed from the surface of Mars has finally arrived! Cheers of relief and jubilation erupt. Styrofoam cups of champagne are raised in celebration.

July 20, 1976, has turned into one of the most important days of Carl Sagan's life. He will soon learn the answers to many of his questions about Mars and, perhaps, succeed in his ultimate quest—to find life elsewhere in the universe.

Carl's parents, Sam and Rachel Sagan

*Chapter* **ONE**

# STARS OVER BROOKLYN

**E**VERYONE TAKES A JOURNEY OF SOME KIND, SOME-
times an imaginary journey to the planets and beyond
and sometimes a real journey across oceans and
continents. Carl Sagan's father, Samuel, was born in
Russia in 1905. At age five, he traveled all the way to
America with his teenaged uncle. Sam Sagan was part
of a large wave of Russian Jewish immigrants who set-
tled in the United States at the turn of the nineteenth
century. They were fleeing religious persecution and
poverty, hoping to find a better life in the New World.

Sam grew up in New York City. He was a gentle
man with flaming red hair, a wry sense of humor, and
a sunny outlook on life. He wanted to become a
pharmacist, but had to drop out of college and go to

work instead. In 1933, Sam met Rachel Molly Gruber at a party and was immediately attracted by her liveliness and charm.

Rachel had been born in New York in 1907. An excellent student and talented writer, she completed a secretarial course at the East New York Business School. By the time she met Sam, she'd been working for several years. Sam and Rachel fell in love and, after knowing each other only a few weeks, got married.

Carl Edward Sagan was born on November 9, 1934. His family lived in the Bensonhurst section of Brooklyn, one of the five boroughs that make up New York City. Like other parts of Brooklyn, Bensonhurst was home to many immigrant families, most of them Italian or Jewish. It was a close-knit community with a friendly, small-town atmosphere. The streets were lined with low-rise apartment buildings, single family homes, and clusters of small businesses.

Carl was born during the Great Depression, a time when jobs were scarce and salaries were low. His parents could afford only a tiny apartment, which grew more crowded with the arrival of another baby six years after Carl. Carl was excited about his new sister and wanted her name to be as much like his as possible. The family named her Carol, but later she chose to be called Cari.

Sam had worked as an usher in a theater but was lucky to find a better-paying job as a cutter in his uncle's clothing factory. Operating a heavy, dangerous power saw, he cut out patterns for women's clothing from enormous stacks of fabric. His workdays were long and exhausting, but he made time to play with Carl and Carol in the evenings.

Like most other married women in the neighborhood, Rachel stayed at home to take care of her family. Although she was a devoted wife and mother, she sometimes missed the stimulation of the working world.

The Sagans couldn't afford to buy much for their children but gave them something money couldn't buy—a love of learning. Although neither Sam nor Rachel had graduated from college, they knew the importance of a good education. Despite their lack of money, they made sure their home was always filled with lots of books. Rachel taught the children to appreciate music, art, and literature, and both she and Sam often read aloud from Shakespeare's plays and other great books.

Even at an early age, Carl's unusual intelligence was obvious. His parents did their best to answer his constant questions and encourage his vivid imagination. In 1939, they took him to the New York World's Fair, which presented a dazzling model of the future made possible by science and technology. Carl was mesmerized by the science exhibits. In one of them, a tuning fork was hooked up to an oscilloscope, a machine that pictured sound as waves on a screen. In another display, a flashlight beam was converted to sound waves by a photocell. Carl was astonished to "see" sound and "hear" light.

Soon after the visit to the fair, Sam taught Carl an important math lesson. He explained the concept of zero and showed how zeros could be used to create very large numbers. Carl was so excited by what he had learned that he begged to write down all the numbers from one to one thousand. Using sheets of scrap cardboard, he began the long task. He had reached only the low hundreds when his mother interrupted, insisting that it was bath time. Carl didn't

*Rachel, Baby Cari (about age two), and Carl (about age nine)*

want a bath—he wanted to get to one thousand. His father worked out a compromise: He would continue writing numbers if Carl would take a bath without complaining. By the time the bath was over, Sam had reached nine hundred. Carl proudly finished the rest of the numbers before going to bed.

As Carl grew older, he went to the local public school and played on the neighborhood streets with his friends. One of his favorite games was stickball, which is similar to baseball. Players used mop or broom handles as bats and a small, pink rubber ball. Everything from cars parked on the street to manhole covers served as bases.

Like most of the kids in the neighborhood, Carl was an avid baseball fan and collected cards and statistics on many players. New York was a baseball-lover's paradise, with three local teams—the Yankees, Giants, and Brooklyn Dodgers. Carl also collected stamps and went to movies with his friends on Saturdays. During the hot, sticky New York summers, the Sagan family escaped to the cool ocean breezes of nearby Coney Island and Atlantic Beach.

Although Carl played with the other children, his thoughts were often far away. When he was five, he began a journey that would change his life as much as the journey to America had changed his father's. Instead of traveling thousands of miles across the ocean in a ship, Carl crossed the vast expanses of space in his imagination. As he gazed up into the nighttime sky over Brooklyn, he stared at the twinkling stars in the velvety blackness and wondered what they were. They seemed more mysterious than either the Sun or the Moon. When Carl asked about them, people told him what he already knew—that stars were lights in the sky.

Carl's parents couldn't answer his questions, but they encouraged him to find out for himself. His mother took him to the nearest branch of the public library. Carl asked the librarian for a book on the stars, and she chose one she thought he would like. To his surprise, it was a book about Hollywood celebrities—

*Cari and Carl at their home in Bensonhurst, Brooklyn, New York*

movie stars. Carl was embarrassed that she had misunderstood him and had to work up the courage to explain that he meant the stars in the night sky. When the librarian finally handed him a book on astronomy, he read it from cover to cover before leaving the library.

What he learned was so astonishing that it captured his imagination forever. The book explained that stars are suns, just like our Sun, but so far away they appear to be only twinkling lights in the sky. Carl, who had never traveled beyond Brooklyn, couldn't grasp the idea of such enormous distances at first. He tried to imagine how incredibly far away the Sun would have to be in order to glimmer like a star rather than shine brightly. Suddenly, the vast size of the universe opened before him.

Magazines like this one fueled Carl's dreams of traveling to Mars one day.

# Chapter **TWO**

# FROM SCIENCE FICTION TO SCIENCE

**C**ARL CONTINUED TO READ EVERYTHING HE COULD find about astronomy. Gradually he realized that since the Sun is a star with planets, other stars must have planets, too. And, like Earth, some of those planets must be inhabited. The possibility that there might be life someplace else in the universe intrigued him. He spent hours trying to picture what living things on other planets might look like, but he was unable to imagine something completely alien. The creatures he pictured were only an assortment of parts from earthly animals and plants.

The world of science fiction was waiting for a young boy who dreamed about traveling to the stars and finding life on other planets. When Carl was ten, a friend introduced him to the space fantasies of Edgar Rice Burroughs. Carl was spellbound by Burroughs's books about Mars and its fictional inhabitants who called their planet Barsoom. The books featured the heroic exploits of John Carter, a courageous warrior and fearless adventurer. In the first book of the series, *A Princess of Mars* (1917), Carter travels to the red planet, but not in a spacecraft. Instead, "I closed my eyes, stretched out my arms . . . and felt myself drawn with the suddenness of thought through the trackless immensity of space. There was an instant of extreme cold and utter darkness. I opened my eyes upon a strange and weird landscape. I knew that I was on Mars."

Carter finds adventure—incredible encounters with violent green giants, vicious eight-legged animals called thoats, other frightening creatures with removable heads, and evil, vengeful warlords. Carter also finds romance—a love affair with the beautiful Dejah Thoris, princess of the Kingdom of Helium.

As Carl read, he noticed that the facts in Burroughs's stories didn't agree with the facts in the astronomy books. It bothered him that Burroughs didn't seem to know much about Mars and that sometimes Carter's adventures were based on details that didn't make any sense.

Carl longed to travel to Mars and explore it. He wanted to see for himself what the two "hurtling moons of Barsoom," as Burroughs called them, looked like from the Martian surface. But no matter what

## THE SCIENCE FICTION OF EDGAR RICE BURROUGHS

Edgar Rice Burroughs (1875–1950) was a prolific writer, best known as the author of *Tarzan of the Apes* (1914), the first of twenty-five Tarzan books. He also wrote many popular science fiction titles. *A Princess of Mars* was the first in the John Carter of Mars series. The other books are *The Gods of Mars; Warlord of Mars; Thuvia, Maid of Mars; The Chessmen of Mars; The Master Mind of Mars; A Fighting Man of Mars; Swords of Mars; Synthetic Men of Mars; Llana of Gathol;* and *John Carter of Mars.* The books are still popular with readers.

kind of wishing Carl did, he remained firmly attached to Earth. There had to be another way.

By 1945, World War II was ending. Carl read in the newspapers about the V-2 rockets the Germans had used to bomb England during the war and how similar rockets might be used for space travel. The British Interplanetary Society had published a study of a rocket that could go to the Moon. "If the moon, then why not Mars?" Carl reasoned.

In the summer of 1945, Carl was in a candy store near his house. The cover of a magazine caught his eye—*Astounding Science Fiction.* A quick glance through the stories inside was enough—he had to own it. Hurrying home, he somehow scraped together enough money, then ran back to the store and bought the magazine. Sinking down onto a bench just outside the store, he was immediately caught up in a fantasy world. Although some of the adventures were not as exciting as those in the Mars books, he realized that the science was more accurate. Carl was hooked and could hardly wait for each month's *Astounding* to arrive at the store.

He read lots of other science fiction magazines and discovered books by remarkable writers such as Jules Verne and H. G. Wells. To keep track of the stories, Carl designed scorecards similar to those he used for baseball. But instead of rating each player on a team, he rated the quality of each story. He found that although the stories were full of new ideas, "Many of them ranked high in asking interesting questions, but low in answering them." Carl was beginning to realize that science fiction was fantasy and that only science could provide reliable answers to his questions. Facts were even more fascinating than fiction.

Carl wanted to become a professional astronomer but thought it would be impossible. He didn't know any astronomers, and none of his family or friends knew any. None of them even had more than a vague idea about what an astronomer did, and getting paid to be an astronomer was beyond anyone's imagination. Carl's grandfather once asked him what he

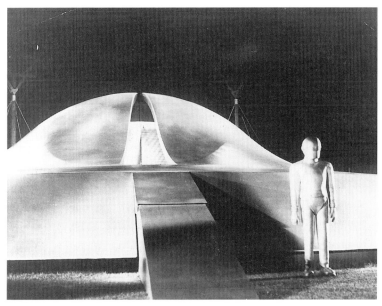

*Although Carl loved watching science fiction films such as* The Day the Earth Stood Still, *facts interested him more than fantasy.*

wanted to be when he grew up. "An astronomer," Carl exclaimed without stopping to think. "Fine," said his grandfather, "but how will you make a living?" Carl figured that he would go into the clothing business with his father. Maybe he would become a salesman—even though he probably wouldn't be very good at it—or take some other dull, uncreative job. Astronomy would have to be his hobby, just as it had been for the fictional John Carter.

As World War II came to an end, the nation's economy was booming. Sam Sagan was promoted from

*Cari (about age six) and Carl (about age thirteen)*

garment cutter to factory manager. His increased
salary allowed the family to leave the crowded apartment and noisy streets of Brooklyn for the tranquility
of a house in Rahway, New Jersey. Eventually, they
were even able to afford the luxury of a horse for
Cari, who loved to ride.

In those days, especially gifted students advanced
through grades at an accelerated pace. Carl entered
Rahway High School at age twelve, where his bril-
liance and wide-ranging interests made him stand out.

Among his classmates, he soon became known as the "walking encyclopedia." As a sophomore, he learned something surprising in biology class—but it had nothing to do with biology. His teacher told him about a well-known astronomer at Harvard University who was paid a salary. Carl was elated by this bit of news, because it meant that it was possible to earn a living doing something he loved.

Carl studied hard. He was eager to learn. But his science and math classes involved mostly dry lectures and mindless memorization. Getting the right answers was all that mattered. Understanding how to get them and thinking creatively were not considered important. Carl maintained his interest in science by reading books and magazines on his own. Although science was his favorite subject, he also enjoyed reading the classics and learning about music and art.

Despite the hours he spent studying, Carl made time for extracurricular activities like basketball and chess. He had lots of friends, including a steady girlfriend. He joined the American Rocket Society, and on weekends he frequently rode the train to its headquarters in Manhattan. There, he chatted with other members and borrowed books by Arthur C. Clarke, one of his favorite science fiction writers.

In Carl's 1951 yearbook photo, he already resembled the handsome man he would become. He was voted "Outstanding Male Student" and "Most Likely to Succeed." High school was almost over. It was time for him to choose a college. His top priority was finding a school with an excellent astronomy program, but he also wanted one with top-rated math and physics departments. And the school had to offer rocket engineering, because—according to all the science fiction Carl had read—an astronomer would have to know how to build his own spaceship.

When considering a college, many high school graduates are as interested in campus life as they are in academics. Does the school have a winning football team? How's the social life? But Carl had other concerns. Among the college catalogs he received was a booklet called "If You Want an Education" sent by the University of Chicago. Many years later, Carl still remembered it. "Inside was a picture of football players fighting on

*Fellow high school students voted Carl "Most Likely to Succeed."*

a field, and under it a caption 'If you want a school with good football, don't come to the University of Chicago.' Then there was a picture of some drunken kids, and the caption 'If you want a school with a good fraternity life, don't come to the University of Chicago.' It sounded like the place for me."

The University of Chicago had an outstanding astronomy department and an impressive science program, and the school had offered Carl a full scholarship. But he worried because it didn't have an engineering school. An astronomer at Princeton University, whom Carl visited to ask for advice, assured him that astronomers didn't have to be engineers as well. Unlike the heroes of science fiction, Carl wouldn't have to build his own rockets in order to study the universe.

Rockets to Mars had been envisioned, but they were not yet a reality. Carl hoped that if he excelled in his studies, he would be selected to travel into space once rockets were built. The University of Chicago would be the perfect place for him to launch his journey to the stars.

*Carl wondered what space aliens looked like, and so did filmmakers. This creature was designed for the 1950s movie* Invasion of the Saucermen.

*Chapter* **THREE**

# REAL SCIENCE

**C**ARL WAS ONLY **16** WHEN HE LEFT HOME AND moved to a new and unfamiliar part of the country. The University of Chicago was near downtown Chicago, a thriving industrial city that had almost as many ethnic neighborhoods as New York. It was the largest city in the Midwest and the second largest in the country. All the cultural attractions of a great city—museums, concerts, restaurants, and theaters— were available. And, by coincidence, Chicago was the birthplace of Edgar Rice Burroughs.

The University of Chicago and Carl were an ideal match—the atmosphere was exciting. Students and professors exchanged ideas and challenged one another to think creatively rather than to repeat memorized facts. Students were required to study a wide range of subjects—everything from literature and art to the sciences. Although Carl was a physics major, he welcomed the chance to learn about philosophy, art, history, and literature. He was eager to learn from the many Nobel Prize-winning professors on the Chicago faculty. And although he hadn't wanted to attend a rah-rah football school, he liked playing sports and served as captain of an intramural basketball team.

During Christmas vacation of his freshman year, Carl met a young biologist who worked in Dr. Hermann Muller's lab at Indiana University. Dr. Muller specialized in genetics, the branch of biology that deals with heredity. He had won the Nobel Prize in 1946 for proving that X rays, a kind of radiation, can cause mutations, or changes, in genes. There are

*American biologist and Nobel Prize winner Professor Hermann J. Muller supported Carl's thoughts on extraterrestrial life.*

many sources of X rays, but not all of them emit enough radiation to cause mutations. An X-ray machine in a doctor's or dentist's office, for instance, delivers a very small dose of radiation, posing little danger of mutation. An exploding star, on the other hand, produces huge amounts of radiation, including X rays. The radiation then travels through space, and some of it reaches Earth. When Earth formed several billion years ago, its atmosphere was thin and didn't provide much protection from radiation. X rays from exploding stars could have reached Earth's surface and caused mutations in the genes of the earliest living things.

The biologist described Dr. Muller's work to Carl, who became convinced that there was a link between the stars and evolution. Carl had never imagined that biology would interest him, but he was intrigued by Dr. Muller's research. When he returned to the University of Chicago after Christmas vacation, he wrote an enthusiastic letter to his new friend at Indiana. The friend showed the letter to Dr. Muller, who was so impressed that he invited Carl to work with him.

Carl spent the next summer in Dr. Muller's lab, studying mutations in fruit flies and getting his first taste of real scientific research. His job included a lot of boring tasks as well as exciting moments of discovery. Dr. Muller, who was interested in learning how life got started on Earth, didn't think that Carl's ideas about extraterrestrial life were silly. Muller became

*Stanley Miller found a way to produce amino acids, the necessary ingredient for the development of life.*

Carl's first mentor and suggested that he study genetics in addition to astronomy. Over the next few years, Dr. Muller kept in touch with Carl, encouraging him to learn about the biology and chemistry necessary for an understanding of genetics. Carl was beginning to understand how the sciences overlap and the importance of studying them all.

Dr. Muller also gave Carl a letter of introduction to Harold Urey, a Nobel Prize-winning chemist at Chicago. Dr. Urey thought Carl showed promise, even though he was only a sophomore. He introduced Carl to Stanley Miller, one of his graduate students. Miller had designed some cutting-edge experiments on the formation of amino acids, the chief components of proteins, an essential part of every living thing.

As if he were filling a helium balloon, Miller pumped a mixture of gases into a large glass container. The mixture contained methane, ammonia, water vapor, and hydrogen—gases that many scientists believe were part of Earth's early atmosphere. When Miller passed an electrical spark—somewhat like a small lightning bolt—through the mixture, amino acids formed on the sides of the container.

Miller was the first person to produce amino acids in this way. He showed that the necessary ingredients for life can form anyplace where the conditions are right. Unfortunately, the chemistry department didn't take his work very seriously—only Dr. Urey defended him. Carl was outraged. How could all those chemistry professors have missed the importance of Miller's work? He had provided a logical explanation for what was possibly the first step in the development of life on Earth: Lightning strikes in Earth's early atmosphere could have caused amino acids to form.

Carl was inspired by his contacts with outstanding scientists like Hermann Muller, Harold Urey, and Stanley Miller. He earned two bachelor's degrees—a liberal arts degree in 1954 and a physics degree in 1955. One year later, he completed a master's degree in physics, then was admitted to the University of Chicago's Ph.D. program in astronomy.

The University of Chicago's Yerkes Observatory in Williams Bay, Wisconsin, houses a 40-inch refractor telescope.

*Chapter* **FOUR**

# LAUNCHING AN ASTRONOMICAL CAREER

**W**HEN CARL ENTERED THE UNIVERSITY OF Chicago's graduate school of astronomy in 1956, he left the big-city sprawl of Chicago for the quiet resort village of Williams Bay, Wisconsin. Williams Bay was the site of the Yerkes Observatory, part of the university's astronomy department and home to the largest refractor telescope in the world. The tiny town was far away from the bright lights and pollution that would interfere with the telescope's ability to provide a clear image of distant objects.

Like all graduate students in the sciences, Carl studied under the guidance of an adviser, a professor in his field of study who assigned him projects and supervised his research techniques. Carl's adviser was

Dr. Gerard Kuiper, a Dutch astronomer and director of the university's two observatories, Yerkes in Wisconsin and McDonald in Texas.

By the 1950s, Dr. Kuiper was the only astronomer in the United States specializing in the study of planets. Toward the end of the nineteenth century, planetary astronomy had been popular. Scientists and the public were excited by the idea that life might exist on Mars and other planets. But enthusiasm gradually faded as the existence of intelligent life remained unproven. Astronomers began looking to the stars and the vast expanse of the universe beyond. The interest in planetary astronomy decreased and almost disappeared.

Dr. Kuiper had made many important contributions to his field. He discovered that carbon dioxide is present in the thin atmosphere of Mars. He discovered two moons—Nereid, which orbits Neptune, and Miranda, which orbits Uranus. He also discovered that Saturn's largest moon, Titan, has an atmosphere and that the atmosphere is composed mostly of methane. As Carl had observed in Stanley Miller's lab, methane can react with other gases to form amino acids. And if amino acids are present, proteins can form and life can evolve. Dr. Kuiper and Carl both believed that planets, especially Mars, were the most likely places to search for alien life.

Carl spent the summer of 1956 with Dr. Kuiper at the McDonald Observatory in Fort Davis, Texas. There, he had his first opportunity to look at Mars

## REFRACTORS AND REFLECTORS

efractors are long, tube-shaped telescopes that use convex lenses to gather light. When light strikes the lenses, it is bent, or refracted, so that it focuses within the tube. The Yerkes telescope in Wisconsin is the largest refractor in the world—it has a lens 40 inches in diameter mounted in a 63-foot-long tube.

Reflectors are also tube-shaped telescopes, but they use a concave mirror to focus light. Astronomers prefer reflectors to refractors, because mirrors can be made much larger than lenses to collect more light. Mirrors are also easier and less expensive to make than lenses. The largest telescope in the world—the Keck telescope in Mauna Kea, Hawaii—is a reflector. Its mirror measures 32 feet in diameter, and its tube is 33 feet long.

The Hubble telescope, launched by the National Aeronautics and Space Administration (NASA) in 1990, is the biggest reflector in orbit—and the best known. Its mirror measures 94 inches in diameter. As it orbits Earth, the Hubble captures images that are free of the distortions caused by Earth's atmosphere. The Hubble also allows scientists to see objects not visible from Earth.

In both refractors and reflectors, gathering light is more important than magnifying images. The lens or mirror must produce clear images that can be photographed or analyzed by computers. To view objects directly through telescopes, astronomers must equip them with eyepieces that magnify images.

through a large, powerful reflector telescope, one of the best in the country. "As it turned out, there were dust storms in both places—Mars and Texas," he recalled. All he saw were some dark and light markings.

Carl was frustrated. "I saw no fine details. It was no big deal. . . . Sitting under a blanket of air forty million miles from the target was not going to tell me much." Forty million miles of empty space was too big a gulf for even the most advanced technology to span.

Carl had studied with two Nobel Prize winners as an undergraduate. Another distinguished scientist entered his life during his graduate years—Dr. Joshua Lederberg, who won the Nobel Prize in 1958. A highly respected professor of genetics at the University of Wisconsin, Lederberg, like some other scientists Carl had met, believed in the possibility of life on other planets. In fact, he invented a word to describe the study of extraterrestrial life, exobiology (later called astrobiology).

Dr. Lederberg had a reputation for being brilliant and forbidding. He was feared among graduate students for his ability to demolish their carefully researched theories with a few stinging remarks. Lederberg knew of Carl's reputation and his dedication to the search for alien life. He had probably read Carl's first published paper, "Radiation and the Origin of the Gene," which explained how radiation may have caused the first DNA molecules to combine and create life. "One day," Carl said, "[Lederberg] called me up out of the blue and said he wanted to see me— said he was interested in extraterrestrial life. I was immensely flattered."

Although he was a geneticist, Dr. Lederberg knew a lot about astronomy. Carl, an astronomer, had studied biology and genetics. The two scientists discussed their ideas. They immediately liked and respected each other, and Dr. Lederberg soon became an important mentor for Carl. Over the years, the two men worked together on many projects.

Dr. Lederberg introduced Carl to other scientists who had begun to consider the possible existence of alien life in the Solar System. He asked Carl to join a committee he headed that was studying ways to search for alien life. In 1960, the newly formed National Aeronautics and Space Administration (NASA) invited Carl to its first exobiology conference. Carl was becoming part of a network of students and professors who shared ideas and would help each other throughout their careers. They came from different areas of science, but most of them had a common goal—searching for an answer to the age-old question: Are we alone in the universe?

Carl had a personal life outside of the classroom and lab. While studying for his master's degree, he had met Lynn Alexander, an undergraduate at the University of Chicago who later became a renowned biologist. The two had a lot in common—both were very intelligent, both were dedicated scientists, and both had strong personalities. When they married in 1957, Carl was 23 and Lynn was 19. Over the next few years, they had two sons, Dorion and Jeremy. Dorion remembers Carl's bedtime stories: "My father used to make up stories about black holes and tell them to my brother and me night after night. In fact, I was probably one of the first people that he experimented on in his attempts to popularize science." Although Carl loved his children, he and Lynn had disagreements. They were divorced in 1963, and the boys remained with their mother.

Carl's gift for telling stories was evident early on. As an undergraduate, he organized a campus lecture series called "The Creation of Life and the Universe," including himself as one of the speakers. The series was a big success, with standing room only in the crowded lecture hall. But many professors criticized Carl, calling the lectures "Sagan's circus" because Carl had a flamboyant personality and speaking style. Many questioned whether Carl was serious about his work.

As a final requirement for his Ph.D., Carl had to write a dissertation, a long paper containing the results of his original research. In his paper, called "Physical Studies of Planets," Carl discussed the atmosphere of Venus and designed models that explained why it has a high temperature. The year was 1960, and Carl, age 25, had earned his Ph.D. in astronomy and astrophysics. He was now called Dr. Sagan—he had credentials as well as a reputation.

He left the University of Chicago and headed west to the University of California at Berkeley, where he spent two years doing research and teaching. While

From left to right: *Cari, Sam, Rachel, and Carl in the backyard of the family home in Rahway, New Jersey, in the mid-1960s*

Carl was in Berkeley, Dr. Lederberg took a position as chairman of the genetics department at the Stanford University School of Medicine in nearby Palo Alto. At his invitation, Carl spent a year there as a visiting assistant professor of genetics.

Then, almost ten years after leaving New Jersey, Carl returned to the East Coast, taking a research position at the Smithsonian Astrophysical Observatory in Cambridge, Massachusetts, in 1962. At the same time, he became a professor of astronomy at Harvard University, also located in Cambridge. He taught there for several years and was very popular with the students.

But his inventive and animated teaching style con-
flicted with the more traditional methods of the other
professors. Harvard didn't offer him a permanent job.

But Cornell University, located in Ithaca, New York,
not only offered him a permanent position but also
asked him to set up its Laboratory for Planetary Stud-
ies. Later, he was appointed the university's David
Duncan Professor of Astronomy and Space Sciences.
In 1968, Carl moved to Ithaca. That year, he married
Linda Salzman, an artist, and they soon had a son,
Nicholas.

At Cornell, Carl had found a new home where he
was free to teach any way he wanted. His methods
were unusual and entertaining. Students would laugh
when he did a sort of hula dance to demonstrate the
unsteady movement of light particles or made strange
noises as he pretended to be a group of molecules es-
caping into space from Earth's atmosphere. In his lab,
he continued the search for extraterrestrial life. One
of his main objectives was to unravel the mystery of
how the building blocks of life—amino acids, proteins,
and DNA—evolved during the early years of Earth's
development. By solving this puzzle, scientists might
learn how life could develop on other planets.

Carl wrote an enormous number of scientific papers
during the 1960s. Many of them discussed two of his
theories that were very controversial. One theory had
been part of his dissertation. It was a new way to explain the strong radio waves given off by Venus, a

phenomenon that had long puzzled astronomers. Carl believed that carbon dioxide in Venus's thick atmosphere trapped the Sun's heat, creating a greenhouse effect—making the planet's surface incredibly hot. He proposed that the radio waves were caused by the high temperatures. But many scientists disagreed. They thought Venus couldn't be hot enough to produce radio waves and instead claimed the waves were caused by an electrically charged layer in the planet's atmosphere. In 1967, a Soviet spacecraft proved that Carl was correct. It measured the temperature from deep inside the atmosphere of Venus—about 850 degrees Fahrenheit, hot enough to produce the strong radio signals.

Carl's other controversial theory concerned changing bright and dark patterns that had long been observed on Mars. In the opinion of many respected astronomers, the patterns were caused by seasonal variations in Martian plant life. Carl disagreed. He figured out that fierce winds raged across Mars's surface, causing dust storms. The blowing dust caused the planet's appearance to change. Later, photos sent back by spacecraft visiting Mars proved that Carl was right once again.

*The north polar ice cap on Mars is clearly visible in this photo taken by the Viking spacecraft.*

# *Chapter* **FIVE**

# MARS MYTHS

**F**OR THOUSANDS OF YEARS, PEOPLE HAVE GAZED UP at the heavens and wondered about the glowing, red-orange disc in the night sky. Its light was steady and didn't twinkle like the stars. To ancient civilizations, the color red meant war or fire. The Romans gave the light a name—Mars—after their god of war.

Throughout the centuries, Earthlings remained fascinated by Mars—it was colorful, it was relatively close, and its appearance seemed to change. Astronomers thought they could see storms, volcanoes, and changing seasons through their telescopes. In 1877, Giovanni Schiaparelli, an astronomer in Milan, Italy, announced that he had observed straight lines crisscrossing the planet's surface. He called them

*In 1877 Giovanni Schiaparelli drew a chart of Mars, showing the markings he named* canali *(canals).*

*canali.* In Italian, canali refers to natural channels, such as riverbeds. But the word was incorrectly translated into English to mean canals—artificial waterways built for irrigation and transportation. Could they have been built by intelligent creatures?

Percival Lowell, an American, found an answer. Although he had a degree in mathematics from Harvard, he became very interested in Schiaparelli's discovery of the "canals" on Mars and decided to become an astronomer. Lowell was rich enough to build his own observatory, and he chose the site carefully. He realized that observatories should be located in isolated deserts or on flat plains or mountaintops rather than in brightly lit cities. In 1884, he built the Lowell Observatory on Mars Hill, in the dry desert air of Flagstaff, Arizona, at an altitude of 7,000 feet.

Lowell spent fifteen years studying Mars and published three books containing his findings. He correctly concluded that it was a dry, barren planet, similar to the desert where his observatory was located. Squinting through his refractor telescope equipped with a 24-inch lens, Lowell saw an ice cap at each pole and lines—Schiaparelli's canali—that stretched from the poles toward the planet's equator. How could the canals be explained? Lowell decided that Mars had once been inhabited by intelligent beings. He assumed that the network of canals must have been designed to carry melting water from the polar ice caps to cities near the equator. The cities' inhabitants would have used the water to irrigate crops.

It was difficult to see Mars clearly because telescopes in those days were not very powerful, and the violent movement of Earth's atmosphere blurred and distorted the view. Some astronomers saw the canals, others saw only streaks or splotches. In fact, Lowell's canals were an optical illusion—Lowell had made one of the biggest blunders in the history of science. But he was a respected astronomer, and his ideas were widely published. The public was intrigued by the idea of extraterrestrial life on the planet closest to Earth.

Inspired by Lowell's canal-building Martians, authors like H. G. Wells and Edgar Rice Burroughs wrote fantasies about time travel and strange, frightening lifeforms on other planets. And if aliens in outer space were intelligent enough to build canals, they could invent spaceships. Stories told how Martians would leave their planet and invade Earth, looking for water and warm climates. In 1938, actor/filmmaker Orson Welles broadcast a radio drama based on H. G. Wells's novel, *The War of the Worlds.* Hundreds of thousands of Americans panicked because they believed the broadcast was a real news report about Martians invading Earth. Some thought the aliens would come in peace. Most feared that Earth and its inhabitants would be destroyed.

The term "flying saucer" was coined when Carl Sagan was in high school. Newspapers then were full of stories about strange craft hovering in the skies. People reported abductions by unearthly creatures who communicated through mental telepathy. Even scientists were influenced by improbable ideas about aliens. In 1960, a Soviet astrophysicist concluded that Phobos and Deimos, the moons of Mars, were not moons at all. He said they were hollow structures that had been manufactured and launched in the distant past by an extinct Martian civilization. More recently, the *Viking* spacecraft transmitted images of a "face" on Mars. Some theories suggested that the features were part of a huge sculpture built by aliens—or even humans who once lived on Mars. (High-powered cameras and advanced techniques of the 1990s showed the "features" to be the result of erosion.)

Since 1950, astronomers have used advanced

*Orson Welles (with arms raised) broadcast a radio program about Martians invading Earth. Many Americans panicked.*

technology to discover new information about the red planet. They have proven that Mars is too cold and its atmosphere too thin to support any sort of complex life-forms. And what about Lowell's canals? Recent missions to Mars revealed that the canals are not straight lines, but countless spots and markings that the human eye connects—an optical illusion. Working on these missions, Sagan recalled, "I found, not altogether to my surprise, not a trace of canals . . . the hundreds of 'classical' canals carrying water from the polar caps through the arid deserts to the parched equatorial cities simply did not exist." Carl's work helped prove beyond a doubt that the canals of Mars were an illusion—that much of the science fiction he loved was based on mistakes and assumptions, not proven scientific facts.

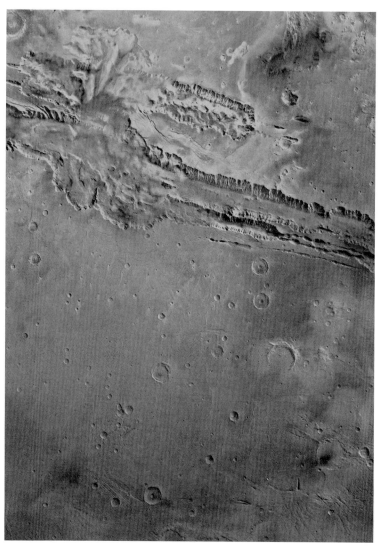

Rugged canyons crisscross the Mars surface, as shown in this photo taken by the Viking orbiter.

*Chapter* **SIX**

# THE MARS
# MISSIONS

**T**HE 1960S WERE A TIME OF GREAT EXCITEMENT AT NASA. The space agency was striving to meet President John F. Kennedy's challenge to land a man on the Moon by the end of the decade. At the same time, it was also carrying out an ambitious program of unmanned space exploration. And Carl Sagan had exactly the right background and skills to make him a valuable member of NASA's planetary exploration team. He was assigned to NASA's Jet Propulsion Laboratory in Pasadena, California, headquarters for the American program to explore the Solar System with unmanned spacecraft. Carl was asked to help design missions to Mars and the other planets, then to interpret the data and images returned by those missions.

As Carl soon learned, trying to send an unmanned probe to explore a planet millions of miles away was an expensive, difficult, and risky operation. It was not unusual for a mission to end in partial or complete failure, no matter how carefully the scientists designed the spacecraft and prepared for every problem they could imagine. Between 1962 and 1973, the United States launched six spacecraft toward Mars. The Soviet Union launched at least eight. Seven of the Soviet probes were lost, missed their targets, or returned little or no information. Two of the American probes failed during launch, but the others accomplished their goals: *Mariner 9* went into orbit around Mars; *Mariners 4, 6,* and *7* didn't orbit or land on Mars, but they passed close enough to send back photos of its surface.

One reason for the success of the Mariner program was NASA's decision to use "twins" for each mission—two identical spacecraft launched about one month apart on slightly different flight paths. With twins, the mission had a chance to succeed even if something went wrong with one of the vehicles. The twins also made economic sense—most of the money, time, and effort were spent to design and build the first spacecraft. It wasn't much more expensive to build a second craft as insurance against a complete mission failure.

The twin probes *Mariners 8* and *9* were launched in 1971. *Mariner 8* failed during launch, but its twin was

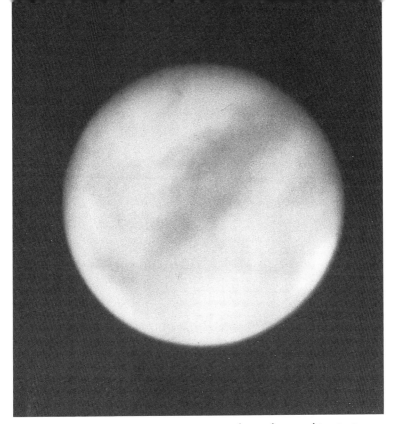

*Carl Sagan once wrote: "Mars moves through our skies in its stately dance, distant and enigmatic, a world awaiting exploration. If we but choose, it waits for us."*

successful beyond the most optimistic predictions of the mission designers at NASA. *Mariner 9* reached Mars and remained in orbit around the planet for almost a year. The spacecraft did not have a lander, but it sent back more than seven thousand photos of the planet's surface taken from orbit.

As a member of the imaging team, Carl helped interpret the photos. He and the other team members watched excitedly as images of Mars appeared on computer monitors in the mission control center. The pictures, made up of thousands of black and white dots, had been stored on magnetic tapes aboard the spacecraft. The information on the tapes was then transmitted, dot by dot, to computers back on Earth. At mission control, the dots were reassembled into images. The *Mariner 9* photos provided more information about Mars than had been gathered in the previous three hundred years.

The *Mariner* photos clearly showed ancient riverbeds, craters, and huge extinct volcanoes, as well as evidence of dust storms and erosion caused by wind and water. The images of dust storms helped prove Carl's theory about the color variations on the surface of Mars. But to Carl, the most exciting photos were the ones showing dried-up riverbeds. They proved that Mars had once had liquid water. Since water is a requirement for life on Earth, similar life-forms might once have existed on Mars. But the *Mariner 9* photos were taken from a great distance and were not detailed enough to show evidence of living organisms. Only a mission that included a lander could provide better information.

NASA's next Mars project involved sending twin spacecraft, *Viking 1* and *Viking 2*, to photograph and analyze the planet's surface and atmosphere and to search for evidence of life. Each spacecraft consisted of an orbiter and a lander.

The failures of the Soviet missions to Mars had taught NASA that flexibility was important. The Soviet spacecraft were completely programmed before their launch and could not respond to unexpected conditions. For instance, one Soviet lander arrived on the surface of Mars during a fierce dust storm. The lander broke down almost immediately. Even if it had continued working, its cameras wouldn't have been able to take good pictures through clouds of blowing dust.

The *Viking* orbiters and landers, on the other hand, could be controlled by scientists on Earth using computers. Instructions could be changed either to correct a problem or to take advantage of an unexpected opportunity. For example, when photos taken by the *Viking* orbiters indicated that the planned landing sites on Mars might be dangerous to the spacecraft, scientists were able to reprogram the landers so that they touched down in safer locations.

NASA especially wanted Carl to work on the *Viking* mission because one of its goals was to search for evidence of extraterrestrial life, and he was one of very few astronomers with a strong background in biology. Carl was assigned to help design the *Vikings'* experiments and equipment. He asked the other team members to consider the possibility that microbes from Earth might contaminate Mars—hitching a ride on the landers. He pointed out that if the experiments found evidence of life, it would be impossible to tell whether the life came from Earth or Mars. Also, Carl said, microbes from Earth could be harmful to Martian life-forms. Carl was skilled at presenting arguments to support his opinions. He finally convinced

## CARL'S REASONS FOR EXPLORING THE RED PLANET

- Mars is the nearest planet that astronauts can explore. (Venus's atmosphere is too hostile.)
- Mars had an Earthlike climate 4 billion years ago. We should study what happened on Mars so that we can try to prevent a climatic disaster on Earth.
- The Martian atmosphere has almost no ozone. By studying Mars, we can understand the consequences of Earth's thinning ozone layer.
- If evidence of life is found on Mars, then life might arise other places in the universe where conditions are right. We might learn what different kinds of life are possible.
- Exploring Mars is ideal for international cooperation and is the best reason for an international space station.
- Mars exploration is a good testing ground for new technologies, such as remote-controlled rovers, remote collection of geologic samples, and the use of virtual reality.
- Mars exploration has strong public support.
- Living conditions on Mars could most easily be made like Earth's, so that the planet could be colonized.
- Mars provides a hopeful dream for future generations.

NASA to spend extra money to sterilize the landers.

*Vikings 1* and *2* were launched one month apart in 1975 and began to orbit Mars in 1976. Both landers reached the surface safely. Although they were designed to last for only three months after touchdown, both landers astonished NASA scientists by continuing to function much longer than planned. The *Viking 1* lander transmitted data for six years; *Viking 2*, for four years. Together, they sent back more than 4,500 photos, as well as an enormous amount of data about weather and surface conditions. The two orbiters sent back an additional 52,000 photos covering 97 percent of the planet's surface. Once again, Carl was a member of the imaging team and helped to interpret the new photos of Mars.

Although the *Viking* missions were extremely successful, they attracted little media or public attention. People expected the missions to find clear evidence of life on Mars. When none was found, most people lost interest. But the *Viking* missions provided scientists with an enormous amount of new information. Mars was becoming almost as familiar as Earth.

Except for Venus, Mars is Earth's closest neighbor. If life could have existed on any other planet in the Solar System, it could have existed on Mars. Billions of years ago, the red planet resembled Earth. It had lots of water—lakes, rivers, and possibly oceans—and a warm atmosphere. Its rocks contain minerals similar to those in Earth's crust, and recent samples suggest that microbes may once have lived there. But Mars has become a planet of deserts, without a drop of liquid water. Intense radiation from the Sun fries its surface. It appears dead.

Mars is farther away from the Sun than is Earth. It takes Earth 365 days to orbit the Sun. Mars takes 687 days. When Earth passes Mars every two years, the planets are closest to each other, about 35 million miles apart. This is the best time for scientists to send spacecraft to Mars and study it through telescopes.

Martian days are only 41 minutes longer than Earth's. And Mars has Earthlike seasons because it tilts on its axis at almost the same angle. But its seasons are almost twice as long because the Martian year is almost twice as long. Seasonal changes are extreme: Winters are long and bitterly cold. Temperatures at the poles drop to minus 200 degrees Fahrenheit. During summer, the surface temperature at the equator can reach a pleasant 80 degrees Fahrenheit. As sunshine warms the air, winds rise, whipping up clouds of pink dust. As the wind speed increases, sometimes up to 300 miles per hour, the dust storms spread. Weeks or months pass before the air clears.

Like Earth, Mars has a permanent ice cap at each pole. But ice on Mars isn't only frozen water. It's thought to be a mix of water and carbon dioxide—sort of like frozen seltzer. In the warm sunshine of summer, some of the ice melts, and the ice caps grow smaller. In winter they grow larger. But even if the ice caps melted completely, Mars would still be drier than the driest desert on Earth.

Mars is only a little more than half the size of Earth. It has about one-ninth the *mass* of Earth, however, which means that the pull of its gravity is weaker—a 100-pound Earthling would weigh only 38 pounds on

## A CLOSE-UP VIEW OF MARS

The orbits of Earth and Mars bring them nearest to each other about every two years. In 2003, Mars will be at its closest approach this century, and the view will be spectacular. Mars will look 50 percent larger than normal and will appear lower in the sky. Whenever it is at its closest, Mars is the brightest light in the night sky, and the details of its surface are easy to see through a telescope. Without a telescope, the planet looks like a red-orange light.

Mars. Walking would be difficult, but leaping would be easy.

Earth's atmosphere is 21 percent oxygen. Mars's atmosphere is 95 percent carbon dioxide, with only traces of oxygen. And Mars has almost no atmospheric pressure because its atmosphere is so thin. An Earthling on Mars would have to wear a space suit that could provide oxygen, protection from extreme cold, and the pressure necessary for the human body to survive.

Mars has clouds and wind and sunshine. It has volcanoes and rolling hills and rocks. It has craters and canyons and deserts. But its geological features are more extreme than Earth's. Most of the planet, especially the Southern Hemisphere, is covered with large

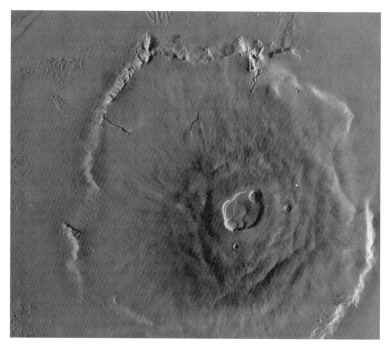

*Olympus Mons, a Martian volcano*

and small craters. One of them is half as wide as the United States! Rocks are scattered about, as if tossed by the waters of raging floods. Vast fields of lava, which flowed from inside Mars for billions of years, cover an enormous area near the equator. Geologists estimated that volcanoes have spread enough lava on Mars's surface to cover an area the size of the United States to a depth of four miles. Four huge volcanoes loom high into the Martian sky. One of them, Olympus Mons, is the largest volcano in the Solar System.

It is 15 miles high—three times as high as Mount Everest—and three times the size of the island of Hawaii. And Mars has the longest, deepest canyon of any planet—Valles Marineris is twice as deep as the Grand Canyon and ten times longer. It would stretch from New York to San Francisco.

Mars has two small moons, named for the sons of Ares, the god of war in Greek mythology. They are Phobos, meaning "fear," and Deimos, meaning "terror." Carl Sagan and a colleague were the first humans to see detailed images of Phobos.

The red colors in Mars's rocks, boulders, soil, and dust come from the large amounts of rusted iron they contain. Mars is a big ball of rust with an iron core. The Martian landscape is a still life in shades of rust—from yellow-brown to orange, from pink to red. There is no grass. There are no trees. There is nothing green on Mars. Millions of miles away is a pale blue dot: Earth.

Carl estimated that a galaxy like Andromeda, above, could contain 100 billion stars and up to 1 million technologically advanced civilizations.

# Chapter **SEVEN**

# IS ANYBODY OUT THERE?

**T**HE *MARINER* AND *VIKING* MISSIONS PROVIDED A lot of information about the geology and climate of Mars, but they didn't address Carl's questions about the possibility of other intelligent life in the universe. While he was studying the *Mariner 9* data, Carl heard about NASA's planned launch of the twin spacecraft *Pioneers 10* and *11*. They were programmed to send back pictures and data from the planets beyond Mars and then become the first man-made objects to leave the Solar System. As soon as he heard, Carl asked NASA for permission to include a message in case the *Pioneer* probes were intercepted by intelligent aliens.

It was not at all certain that NASA would agree to Carl's unusual request. Several years earlier, Carl and a Russian astrophysicist had coauthored a book, *Intelligent Life in the Universe*. It contained a serious discussion of the possibility that intelligent extraterrestrials existed and could be contacted. The book helped make the idea of searching for other intelligent beings more acceptable to the scientific community, but trying to contact extraterrestrials wasn't yet considered mainstream scientific research. And there was another problem. The *Pioneer* mission was almost ready for launch. At such a late date, any change would be difficult and expensive. To Carl's amazement, NASA officials quickly approved his idea. He had only a short time to decide what kind of message to send.

It seemed obvious to Carl that the message would have to be written in the only language that could be understood throughout the universe—the language of science. And it would have to include a few basic scientific facts that would be familiar to any intelligent alien. Carl and a colleague from Cornell, Frank Drake, worked out a first draft in only a few hours. They drew a diagram showing two different forms of the hydrogen atom, which is found everywhere in the universe. They also drew a diagram of the Solar System, including the flight path of the *Pioneer* spacecraft. A third drawing showed how to locate the Solar System in the Milky Way Galaxy.

Carl also asked his second wife, Linda Salzman, to add a more personal message from Earth. She drew two nude figures, a man and a woman. The man's right hand was raised in a sign of peaceful greeting. Linda's drawings and the scientific information were engraved on two gold-coated aluminum plaques. It took just three weeks from the time NASA approved Carl's idea for the plaques to be designed and made. Only six by nine inches, the plaques were smaller than pieces of loose-leaf paper.

*Pioneer 10,* launched in 1972, and *Pioneer 11,* launched in 1973, became famous because of Carl's two golden plaques. Many people praised him for sending an uplifting "message to the stars." But he also received some angry letters criticizing him for sending the first "smut" into space. And some feminists complained that the man had his hand raised, but the woman wasn't doing anything. Even Carl wasn't totally pleased with the pictures because the humans on the plaques looked too Caucasian. Linda had included Asian and African facial features in her original drawings, but these distinctions were lost during the engraving process. Despite their flaws, Carl's plaques continue their journey and will last for hundreds of millions of years in the cold emptiness of space.

Carl realized that there was almost no chance an intelligent alien would someday find and read one of his messages. His real purpose was to encourage people on Earth to look at themselves from a cosmic viewpoint—to see themselves as citizens of the universe. He hoped that humans might one day forget their differences and work together for the good of the entire planet.

Carl continued to believe in the possibility of intelligent extraterrestrial life, however. When NASA announced its plans for *Voyager*, a mission to Jupiter and Saturn and beyond, he asked to include a more elaborate message than the one on the *Pioneer* plaques. Once again, NASA officials accepted his proposal, and he assembled a team to begin work on a disc containing both images and sounds from Earth. The team's creative director was Ann Druyan, a novelist and television writer whom Carl had known for several years and who shared his enthusiasm for science.

This time, Carl wanted to send a portrait of Earth rather than just a scientific message. He hoped to show Earth's position in the universe, its diversity of life, and the richness of human culture. Each gold-plated copper disc contained 115 images and a variety of sounds. The discs could be played like phonograph records and were stored in protective aluminum covers on the outside of each *Voyager*, along with the cartridges and needles needed for operation. Instructions for playing the discs and for determining where the spacecraft came from were engraved on the covers.

The twin *Voyagers* were launched in 1977. Like *Mariner 9* and *Vikings 1* and *2*, the *Voyagers* surpassed all expectations. Both spacecraft sent back thousands of close-up shots of Jupiter and Saturn. Mission scientists made many discoveries, including three new

At a news conference, Carl discussed the possibility that the planet Jupiter might harbor some form of life.

moons orbiting each planet and unexpected rings around Jupiter. As *Voyager 1* left the Solar System, its cameras were turned on for a last look toward home. Its farewell picture was a family portrait of the Sun with six of its nine planets—Venus, Earth, Jupiter, Saturn, Uranus, and Neptune.

Although *Voyager 2* had serious mechanical problems after it was launched, engineers worked around them by using computers. The long-distance repairs were so successful that the spacecraft was reprogrammed after it flew past Jupiter and Saturn and was instructed to go on to Uranus and Neptune. Its cameras, too, were turned on one last time. They sent back the best photos ever taken of the mysterious planets at the edge of the Solar System. Both *Voyagers* are still transmitting data as they continue their separate journeys into outer space.

Although pleased with NASA's willingness to include messages with the *Pioneer* and *Voyager* probes, Carl realized that attaching messages to spacecraft was not an effective way to contact intelligent extraterrestrials. Carl's friend, Frank Drake, had already spent many years on the "search for extraterrestrial intelligence" (SETI). Using a more promising method, he had been scanning the heavens with a radio telescope, listening for the kind of signal that only an intelligent civilization could produce.

In 1974, Frank decided to try a different approach. Instead of listening for alien transmissions, he sent a powerful signal out into space, using a huge radio telescope at the Cornell observatory in Arecibo, Puerto Rico. The signal contained a message written in binary code, the language of computers. The message was very similar to the one on the *Pioneer* plaques, but there were no naked people.

The message was beamed toward a dense cluster of stars called M13, about 21,000 light-years, or 126 quadrillion (126,000,000,000,000,000) miles, from Earth. If the message is ever received by intelligent extraterrestrials capable of sending back a reply, Earth will wait a long time for the response. The round trip of 252 quadrillion miles will take at least 42,000 years. Because of the enormous distances involved, sending a message to a single galaxy and waiting for a reply is very inefficient. Listening for signals from many different galaxies is a much more effective way to make contact.

In 1975, Carl joined Frank to listen in on the nearby

Andromeda Galaxy. Using an equation Frank developed, Carl estimated that a galaxy like Andromeda, with 100 billion stars, could have up to 1 million technologically advanced civilizations. Frank tuned the telescope's receiver to a very quiet frequency (one with little background radiation), perfect for an extraterrestrial who wanted to make contact. But the men heard only static. Carl was surprised and disappointed. With so many possibilities, how could there be no signal?

In 1980, Carl and Bruce Murray, a friend who was head of JPL, founded the Planetary Society. Its goals were to encourage space exploration and the search for extraterrestrial life and to promote cooperation among nations for exploring outer space. The new organization, open to anyone with an interest in space, signed up 20,000 members in its first year. One of the Planetary Society's main projects was a radio astronomy search—24 hours a day, 365 days a year—for extraterrestrial broadcasts. It was named Project META, or Mega-channel Extraterrestrial Assay, because the astronomers monitored millions of radio channels at a time. Over a five-year period, they picked up 37 signals that seemed promising, but none of them turned out to be the hoped-for message.

Carl holds a model of the planet Venus, one of the many models he used to explain the universe.

## Chapter **EIGHT**

# A SUPERSTAR
# IS BORN

**M**ANY PEOPLE AVOID STUDYING SCIENCE BECAUSE they believe that even the simplest scientific concepts will be too difficult to understand. And when people are ignorant about science, they are more easily fooled by con artists and quacks. Carl Sagan was determined to expose the false claims of pseudoscience (fake science), and he spent a great deal of time explaining real science in a way that everyone could understand.

He publicly criticized the ideas that people could contact the dead during seances or predict behavior from astrological charts. He discouraged belief in miracle cures, out-of-body experiences, and psychic predictions. He believed that he might someday contact intelligent extraterrestrials but refused to accept wide-spread stories of UFO sightings and alien abduc-tions—no one had ever produced physical proof that they had happened.

Carl wasn't born knowing how to think like a scien-tist—it was a skill he had to learn. In school, Carl learned about the scientific method: Scientists who have a question to answer start by gathering facts. Then they think up several possible answers, called hypotheses, each of which must be tested against the facts. If several hypotheses fit the facts, scientists usu-ally choose the simplest. A complicated hypothesis is considered only when every other possibility has been eliminated. The scientific method is the basis for all valid scientific research and writing.

Carl gave the scientific method a special name—the "baloney detection kit." A good baloney detection kit, he said, contained tools for skeptical thinking—know-ing how to construct a well-reasoned explanation and how to recognize a false one. Carl had written hun-dreds of papers about his research. They appeared in professional journals and were highly regarded by his peers in the various fields of science. But Carl was concerned about "scientific illiteracy" among the gen-eral public, and he began writing books and articles about science for ordinary people.

He wrote articles for popular magazines like *National Geographic* and *Parade,* a Sunday newspaper supplement reaching more than 80 million people each week. With Annie Druyan as a frequent coauthor, he wrote about subjects ranging from space missions to how life began to the prehistoric origins of sports. He also wrote the "Life" entry for the *Encyclopedia Britannica.*

Carl returned to several key ideas over and over again in his writing: He promoted science as the best way to understand the world and argued against the claims of pseudoscience and superstition. He described the benefits of space exploration and urged people to support funding for it. He laid out the case for the existence of intelligent extraterrestrial life and encouraged his readers to think of themselves as citizens of the universe. And he described the delicate balance of Earth's ecosystems, warning of possible environmental disaster if humans didn't take responsibility for their planet.

Carl wanted his readers to enjoy learning about science. He had a special ability to explain difficult ideas clearly and to make science come alive. His writing was also very personal—he didn't hesitate to include his opinions on political and religious issues as well as scientific ones.

In 1973, Carl wrote a book called *The Cosmic Connection: An Extraterrestrial Perspective.* In it, he describes what is already known about the planets and the stars and speculates about the possibility of contacting intelligent extraterrestrials. In *The Dragons of Eden,* written in 1977, Carl discusses the evolution of human intelligence and the human brain. Carl took a professional risk writing the book. Although he had taken many courses in biology and genetics at the University of Chicago, he hadn't specialized in those subjects. Some scientists were angry with him for daring to write about areas of science other than his own. But the critics—and, more important, the public—disagreed. *The Dragons of Eden* became a best-seller and won the Pulitzer Prize, one of the most important honors in the book world.

*Carl used a giant model of the Solar System to explain the orbits of the planets.*

Carl Sagan was in love with science and wanted everyone to share in its awesome wonder. His big chance came in 1972 with an appearance on *The Tonight Show*, one of the most popular shows on television, with more than 15 million viewers tuning in five nights a week. Most of the show's guests were actors, comedians, musicians, and other performers. The appearance of a scientist was indeed unusual. Carl was given only five minutes at the end of the show to plug his new book, *The Cosmic Connection*. But in that short time he was so amusing and talked about such interesting topics, including UFOs and extraterrestrial life, that he made an unforgettable impression. Host Johnny Carson immediately invited him back.

On his next visit, three weeks later, Carl again captivated the audience. His presentation was dramatic. In a deep, theatrical voice he talked about the history of the universe and the beginnings of life. And he didn't look like a scientist: He was over six feet tall and slender. He wore his thick dark hair long and slightly shaggy. He was handsome, his face animated by a dazzling smile and sparkling green eyes. He was casually dressed in a turtleneck and corduroy jacket. "When his [talk] ended," one reviewer said, "100,000 teenage listeners must have vowed on the spot to become astronomers."

The audience loved Carl. Not only was he entertaining, but he could also explain complicated scientific ideas so they were easy to understand. "My only secret in being able to talk to others about science is to remember what it was like when I didn't understand whatever it was we were talking about," Carl explained. He appeared so often on *The Tonight Show* during the 1970s and 1980s that even when he wasn't there, Johnny Carson could make an audience laugh just by putting on a black wig and talking in a deep voice about "billions and billions" of stars in the universe. Carl often pointed out that he never actually used the phrase "billions and billions," but people continued to associate it with him.

As a media star, Carl realized that television was the most powerful means of communication. Along with his books, he could use TV to teach the public about the universe and the exciting possibilities of space exploration. Carl and Gentry Lee, a close friend and coworker at the JPL, decided to create a television show. But when they teamed up with a Los Angeles public television station, their modest plan expanded into a thirteen-part weekly series called *Cosmos.*

The series would cover many of the subjects Carl wrote about in his books—the exploration of planets, the origin of life on Earth, and the search for life in this galaxy and beyond. But *Cosmos* would also include other topics that interested Carl, like history, literature, and religion. He would be the writer and the only person on-screen, visible almost constantly in every episode.

*Carl was fond of using teaching aids. Here he holds a large model of the planet Mars.*

Carl knew that *Cosmos* would have to be entertaining as well as educational. He, the producer, and the crew wanted to dramatize science on television using techniques found, at that time, only in the movies. They created seventy spectacular special effects. The first segment began with a twenty-five-minute spaceship ride to Earth from eight billion light-years away. The ship zoomed past giant wheeling galaxies, exploding supernovae, quasars, pulsars, and a Martian dust storm before finally landing in ancient Egypt. Viewers also toured the ice rings of Saturn, saw a lightning display on Jupiter, and landed on Venus. Other special effects made it look as if Carl were sliding into a bottomless black hole, strolling through a human brain with electrical impulses flashing around him, and visiting a pulsating model of the DNA molecule.

*Carl used a* Viking *lander to explain experiments conducted on Mars.*

In all, *Cosmos* was filmed on forty locations in twelve countries. It took three years to make and cost $8 million. More than 150 people were involved in its creation, including animation experts from the JPL and a special effects team that had worked on the *Star Wars* movie. *Cosmos* was the most ambitious project ever produced by public television.

Carl's personal life changed dramatically during the years that *Cosmos* was produced. He moved across the country from Ithaca to Los Angeles, and his aging parents, Sam and Rachel, moved there to live with him. Shortly after filming began, Carl found out that his father had lung cancer. Despite the project's hectic schedule, Carl insisted on taking time to be with the father he loved so much. Unfortunately, Sam died less than a year later.

Carl's marriage to Linda also ended around this time. When Carl moved to Los Angeles, Linda and Nicholas, their ten-year-old son, stayed behind in Ithaca. The couple divorced in 1981. By then, Carl had become so famous that the divorce got a lot of publicity. Shortly after, he married Annie Druyan. They had fallen in love when working on the *Voyager* recordings. Annie helped write *Cosmos* and coauthored many other projects with Carl.

Carl had invested three years of hard work. Public television and others had invested millions of dollars. They had all taken an enormous risk on a project that could have been a failure. But *Cosmos* became a huge success for two reasons: It turned scientific facts into a fascinating story, and it attracted a larger audience than any other series in the history of public television. Since it first aired, *Cosmos* has been seen by more than 500 million people in sixty countries. A book with the same title, published as a companion to the show, has sold over one million copies. It is the best-selling science book ever published in the English language.

Carl had been a famous scientist before *Cosmos*. Afterward, wherever he went people recognized him and asked for his autograph. Never before in the history of science or mass media had a scientist's name, face, and voice been so famous. He was called "America's most effective salesman of science," "the prince of popularizers," "the cosmic explainer," and "a scientist superstar."

In 1980, the year that *Cosmos* was first televised, Carl and Annie wrote a 120-page proposal for a movie. Then Carl wrote a book based on the proposal. Five years later, the book was published. Seventeen years later, the movie was released. Both were called *Contact*. Carl had written the book for the same reason that he appeared on television—to bring science to millions of non-scientists.

*Contact* is science fiction but is based on scientific fact. Carl described it as "an account—consistent with the best scientific probabilities—of what contact between humans and an extraterrestrial civilization would be like." Although most movies that deal with science usually get it wrong, Carl made sure that *Contact* got it right. *Contact* is about SETI, the search for extraterrestrial intelligence by radio astronomers. The aliens in the movie aren't monsters—they don't look like weird reptiles or deformed humans—and they don't want to destroy Earth. The main character, a young radio astronomer named Ellie, hears the first radio signal ever from another planet and heroically

*Actress Jodie Foster in a scene from the film* Contact.

leaves Earth to search for its source. Carl said that Ellie is based on Annie. Annie says that Ellie is more like Carl.

The book was Carl's first and only work of fiction. Like his nonfiction books, it became a best-seller. And the movie, starring Jodie Foster and released after Carl's death, was a box-office hit.

*Carl protested against the use of nuclear arms.*

## Chapter **NINE**

# SPEAKING FOR PLANET EARTH

**W**HEN CARL WAS YOUNG, HIS PARENTS TAUGHT him to care about and help people who were less fortunate than he. As an adult, he spoke out on political and social issues that were important to him. In the 1960s, he demonstrated against the Vietnam War, and he worked in the Civil Rights movement, volunteering to teach science to black students in Alabama. Many female scientists remember him as one of the first male scientists to regard them as equals.

During the 1980s, Carl became involved in efforts to influence government policy on environmental issues. One of his main concerns was the possibility of nuclear war. His research convinced him that even a war fought with a limited number of nuclear weapons might cause a worldwide environmental disaster and the extinction of many species, including humans.

A science fiction story Carl had read as a child first made him aware of the catastrophic threat posed by nuclear weapons. The story was about time travel into the future, after a terrible nuclear war had devastated Earth. Many years later, Carl's research on the Martian climate led to an insight about how a nuclear war could cause a global disaster. He observed that dust thrown up by seasonal storms on Mars blocked sunlight and greatly cooled the planet's surface. Along with other scientists, he began to wonder about the long-term effects that dust and other pollution from nuclear explosions might have on Earth's climate.

Carl asked four other scientists—Richard Turco, Brian Toon, Thomas Ackerman, and James Pollack— to help him study the environmental problems that could be caused by a nuclear war. The group called itself TTAPS, an acronym using the first letters of their five last names. It was a good choice, since taps is the military bugle melody played at the end of the day and at funerals.

To find out how smoke, dust, and radiation from nuclear explosions might change climate, TTAPS used computer models as well as data from actual events such as large forest fires and volcanic eruptions. The five scientists also researched the effects of poisonous gases, radioactive fallout, and ultraviolet light.

While TTAPS was studying the possible effects of

Carl told the Senate Armed Services Committee that a nuclear war could create a "nuclear winter" effect. Billions might die of starvation. He used a photograph of Earth to illustrate a nuclear war viewed from space.

nuclear war, a Nobel Prize-winning physicist at Berkeley, Luis Alvarez, was investigating the extinction of the dinosaurs 65 million years ago. He proposed that an extreme climate change had wiped out the dinosaurs, along with many other species. Based on

*Carl feared that a nuclear explosion would destroy life on Earth.*

evidence found in rock layers dating to the last days of the dinosaurs, Alvarez suggested that a large asteroid had hit Earth, throwing huge amounts of smoke and dust into the air. By blocking out sunlight, the smoke and dust drastically lowered Earth's temperature and caused many plants to die. Animals that didn't freeze to death starved. Even though many scientists ridiculed Alvarez's theory, Carl was convinced he was right. He believed that a nuclear war could have the same consequences as an asteroid impact.

In 1983, TTAPS published an article describing its research and conclusions. In addition to the immediate destruction and death caused by a nuclear bomb and its radioactive fallout, a nuclear explosion would ignite everything flammable within 10 miles of the blast site, the scientists argued. Dust, soot, and smoke would be thrown high into the atmosphere, forming a dense cloud that would eventually cover the globe. The cloud would last for years, preventing sunlight from reaching Earth. Without light, plants would die and animals would either starve or freeze to death, just as they had when the dinosaurs became extinct.

The TTAPS theory of a catastrophic "nuclear winter" was published in a popular book in 1984. It attracted the attention of government officials as well as the public. Military leaders from the Department of Defense interviewed Carl to learn more about his ideas. Some military officials disagreed with Carl's predictions, but the issue had been brought to their attention. Many scientists also challenged the conclusions reached by TTAPS. They argued that the group had used only worst-case numbers to calculate the effect of dust and soot on the global climate. Sagan and his colleagues admitted that their predictions of nuclear winter were based on untested assumptions about nuclear weapons and imperfect computer models of the

Earth's atmosphere. But they believed they were right to warn the government and the public about the possibility of a nuclear catastrophe. Although the nuclear winter theory is controversial, it has helped shape public opinion about the use of nuclear weapons.

In 1986, Carl and Annie helped organize a protest near an underground nuclear test site in Nevada. During the protest, they saw the needle on their Geiger counter, a device for measuring radiation, suddenly jump. Although they hadn't felt anything, they were shocked when they realized what the Geiger counter reading meant. A nuclear bomb had just been detonated under the ground. Along with more than one hundred other protesters, Carl and Annie were arrested and charged with trespassing on government property. They were quickly released, and all criminal charges against them were later dropped. In 1987, the couple organized another protest at the same Nevada site. It was the largest demonstration ever held there, and, once again, hundreds of protesters were arrested for nonviolent civil disobedience.

Carl was concerned about other threats to the global environment, especially holes in the ozone layer and a rapidly increasing greenhouse effect. Ozone is an invisible gas that surrounds Earth, preventing large amounts of ultraviolet radiation from reaching its surface. Too much ultraviolet radiation can cause skin cancer, damage eyesight, and make the human immune system less able to fight off disease. Carl also believed that large amounts of ultraviolet radiation might kill off tiny organisms called plankton, the foundation of the food chain in the oceans. Without plankton, all marine life would die.

Years before, Carl's research on the atmosphere of Venus had proved that a runaway greenhouse effect had made Earth's neighbor a fiery inferno. He was afraid that humans might be causing dangerous global warming by releasing huge amounts of greenhouse gases—from car exhaust, factory smokestacks, and other sources—into the atmosphere. Perhaps Earth might become another Venus, Carl warned. By lecturing and writing about environmental issues, he hoped to make people consider the effect of their actions on Earth's delicately balanced ecosystems.

THE PLANETARY SOCIETY

NATIONAL SPACE SOCIETY

*Carl used every opportunity to talk about space and about ways to protect our planet's fragile ecosystems.*

*Chapter* **TEN**

# AT HOME IN THE UNIVERSE

**A**FTER *COSMOS* WAS COMPLETED, **CARL AND ANNIE** moved back to Ithaca, near the Cornell University campus. Despite his international celebrity, Carl continued his academic work at Cornell, where he remained a professor of astronomy and space sciences. Each year, he taught a course called "Our Home in the Universe" or led seminars such as "Critical Thinking" and "Planetary Exploration and the Origin of the Universe." He also remained director of the Laboratory for Planetary Studies and the David Duncan Professor of Astronomy and Space Sciences.

Annie gave birth to Alexandra, nicknamed Sasha, in 1983. Sam followed eight years later. When Carl played with the children, space fantasies would often creep into their games. As little boys, Dorion and Jeremy, Carl's sons from his first marriage, heard stories about black holes. When Nicholas, Carl's son from his second marriage, was young, Carl pretended to be a creature from Ganymede, a moon of Jupiter. The creature's goofy smile and odd hopping walk "reduced Nick to side-splitting laughter," Annie recalls. And she remembers how Carl played with Sasha and Sam, whirling them in the air and yelling "unidentified flying baby."

The Sagans' large, comfortable house was a gathering place for their extended family. Rachel, Carl's mother, lived with them until her death in 1982, and Annie's parents lived across the street. Dorion and Jeremy often visited. When he had time, Carl watched movies and sporting events. He was passionate about football and basketball, especially the New York Knicks. Before dinner, Carl and Annie often relaxed by playing a card game called pinochle. Family dinners were a time for lively discussions on a variety of topics. Sasha, ignoring her father's reputation as a brilliant thinker, often challenged his opinions.

The house's many windows looked out onto a forest of pine and oak trees. In good weather, Carl and Annie often sat on an outdoor deck that backed onto a deep gorge with a sixty-foot waterfall. With the soothing sound of the waterfall in the distance, they collaborated on various projects, discussing and editing what each had written. Throughout the 1980s and

*Carl and his wife, Annie*

early 1990s, they continued to write articles for *Parade* magazine, explaining difficult scientific concepts and talking about the environment and nature's beauty. In 1996, Carl wrote a book called *The Demon-Haunted World: Science as a Candle in the Dark*. It was a collection of essays about one of his favorite topics—the "boneheaded" notions of pseudoscience contrasted with the importance of science and its application in everyday life.

Carl's fame as a science popularizer hurt his professional reputation, however. Throughout his career, some scientists looked down on him for what they believed was a waste of time—teaching science to ordinary people. And many scientists didn't want science to be simplified. Carl, obviously, disagreed. He reasoned that since most scientific research depended on government funding, it was important for people to understand what their taxes were supporting. The more they understood, the more likely they would be to support scientific research and programs. He also believed that scientists were good role models for children.

One morning in 1994, Annie noticed a bruise on Carl's arm. He went to the doctor for some routine blood tests. When the results showed that something might be wrong, more tests were done. The diagnosis was myelodysplasia, a rare blood disease affecting the bone marrow. Carl's red and white blood-cell counts were extremely low. If untreated, he would die. The only known treatment was a bone marrow transplant, which required a donor with matching bone marrow. Luckily, Carl's sister, Cari, was a match. In 1995, Carl went to the Fred Hutchinson Cancer Research Center in Seattle, Washington, for the transplant. The whole family moved there to be with him during the many weeks of painful, exhausting procedures.

After several months, Carl seemed to have recovered,

but in December the myelodysplasia returned. He went back to Seattle for another transplant, then returned to Ithaca to celebrate Thanksgiving with his family. When the second transplant was unsuccessful, he underwent yet another. Thousands of people around the world prayed for his recovery. But nothing helped. On December 20, 1996, Carl died of pneumonia, a complication of his illness. He was 62 years old.

Carl holds one of the Voyager discs containing Earth sounds and pictures sent as an introduction of sorts to whoever might be living in outer space.

# EPILOGUE

Annie and the children still live in Ithaca, in the house overhanging the gorge. Their lives continue as before. The house remains a gathering place for family and friends and is the scene of many lively discussions. "His absence at those conversations is one of the things we all miss very much," Annie says.

Carl's legacy lives on through his family. He was very proud of his children, believing in their dreams just as his parents had believed in his. Dorion is a science journalist and writer. He is the coauthor of several books with his mother, Lynn (Alexander) Margulis, a well-known biologist who specializes in the study of microbes. Dorion's son, Tonio, is a gifted artist and Carl's first grandchild. Jeremy is a musician who creates computer software used for composing music. Nicholas is a screenwriter and story editor who has written several acclaimed episodes for the *Star Trek* television series. Sasha is a talented poet who volunteers as a reading tutor and wants to become an actress. And Sam is described by his mother as "the spitting image of Carl"—tall and slender, with dark hair and dark eyes. He plans to be a comedian when he grows up.

Carl's last book was *Billions and Billions*. He was still healthy when he began writing it, but wrote the last pages from his hospital room. It includes essays on religion, the environment, nuclear weapons, astronomy, and, at the end, death. After he died, Annie wrote an epilogue for the book. It is a love letter that movingly describes his last days—his brave battle against his illness, his courage facing death, and the emotions of the family, united in love for him. She also helped finish the movie version of *Contact*, which was released in July 1997.

These days, Annie is working on several science series for public television, as well as a possible rebroadcast of *Cosmos*. Her lectures and seminars, as well as the television series, reflect Carl's beliefs. She says, "One of his greatest gifts was his commitment to the truth. Not what's going to make you feel good, less afraid, less small, more central to the working of the universe. But to what's true."

Annie is proudest of a project that will provide health care to some of New York City's most disadvantaged children. She has worked hard to make the Carl Sagan Discovery Center, the first children's hospital in the Bronx, a reality. The hospital will embody Carl's belief that humans are inseparable from the rest of the universe. All sick children will be treated, even if they lack money or insurance coverage. But the hospital has a more ambitious goal—to change lives. Every bed will have an interactive computer hookup that will teach patients about science and nature and explain the importance of caring for Earth. Annie hopes that children who come to the hospital with diseases or injuries will not only be cured but will

## MURMURS OF EARTH

The *Voyager* discs include a wide range of images: drawings of the Solar System and a DNA molecule; photographs of a father and daughter, a nursing mother, rush-hour traffic, a Balinese dancer, dolphins, and a flying insect among flowers.

The discs also contain a variety of sounds including the roar of surf, the rumble of thunder, the songs of birds, and Carl's joyous laugh; greetings in 60 human languages and one in humpback-whale language; and 90 minutes of music from around the world, including classical symphonies, rock-and-roll hits, and traditional folk songs.

In an attempt to capture one person's energy, the discs also contain an hour-long recording of the electrical activity of Annie Druyan's brain, heart, eyes, and muscles.

also learn skills that will give them a better future.

Carl's scientific legacy also lives on in his former students. He was an exceptional teacher who was generous with his time. His seminars were filled with new ideas that any interested student could use as the basis for his or her own research projects. And he went out of his way to find opportunities for his students to work on space missions or with organizations such as the Jet Propulsion Laboratory. Even students who didn't become professional scientists were inspired by his teaching. Bill Nye, "the Science Guy" on public television, took an astronomy course from Carl and after graduation consulted with him about a career in science communication. Diane Ackerman, a noted writer and poet, took Carl's basic course about planets in order to write more accurate poems about them. The poet and the scientist became lifelong friends, sharing a view of the universe from the perspectives of both art and science.

Dr. Steven Squyres, another former student, leads a NASA team designing an unmanned Martian rover scheduled to land on the planet in 2003. The rover will drill into Mars's hard volcanic rock and send samples back to Earth. Scientists hope to find Martian microbes, either living or dead, that would prove the existence of alien life. Squyres remembers Carl's class on the physics of the planets as "the best course I ever took in my life."

Dr. Christopher Chyba, another protégé, is chairman of a NASA committee drafting plans for an unmanned spacecraft that will orbit Europa, a large moon of Jupiter. An underground ocean may lie beneath Europa's icy, cracked surface. NASA wants to know if the ocean exists and whether it contains alien life. Dr. Chyba says that one of the most important lessons Carl taught him was the value of curiosity.

Daniel Goldin, NASA's top administrator, never took a class from Carl. But shortly after coming to NASA in 1992, Goldin began consulting with Carl about the space agency's future. They had dozens of meetings over the next four years, the last one just two weeks before Carl's death. As a result, Goldin became convinced that he "had to develop a vision and a strategy for Mars." Twenty years before, Carl had argued that unmanned exploration was the cheapest and most efficient way to gain scientific knowledge about Mars and the other planets. He'd also envisioned using a "better *Viking*" that included a roving vehicle.

Following Carl's vision, in 1993 NASA began to develop a new series of Mars missions featuring cheaper, simpler, and faster spacecraft. The original plan was to launch an unmanned orbiter and lander every other year, each time Mars and Earth are closest to each other. The program was intended to continue for at least sixteen years and involve more than twelve spacecraft, thousands of scientists, and billions of dollars. The series began in March 1996 with the launching of the *Mars Global Surveyor*, followed by *Mars Pathfinder* with its roving vehicle, *Sojourner*. These spacecraft successfully completed their missions, but by the time *Pathfinder* landed in July 1997, Carl had died. The lander was renamed in his honor.

There have been some failures: *Mars Climate Orbiter*, launched in December 1998, crashed. *Mars Polar Lander*, launched in January 1999, reached Mars but was never heard from. NASA has suspended the Mars missions while it reconsiders its cheaper, simpler, faster plan.

The search for extraterrestrial intelligence (SETI)

continues. The work was carried out by NASA until 1993, when Congress cut funding for the program. In 1994, Frank Drake and others founded the SETI Institute, which, with money from private sources, continues the search using a worldwide network of radio telescopes. Donations have also funded the institute's honorary Carl Sagan Chair for the Study of Life in the Universe, now held by Chris Chyba. The first full-time professorship for SETI research has recently been established at the University of California at Berkeley. The university maintains an array of ten radio telescopes in Northern California and plans to build a much larger network during the next few years. ET hasn't phoned yet. Earth is still waiting for contact.

Before life evolved on Earth, before there was an Earth, all the elements necessary for life could be found in the stars. Billions of years ago, a distant star exploded, and its remains hurtled into space. The Solar System, including Earth, formed out of this debris. The elements from the exploding star combined to create the molecules that are the building blocks of life on Earth. Carl often said that we are "starstuff."

In his 1994 book, *Pale Blue Dot,* Carl questioned whether life on Earth could have developed from microscopic Martian organisms. As the Solar System developed, asteroids and comets often smashed into the planets, causing chunks of rock to fly into space. Rocky debris from Mars may have contained tiny life-forms, and it may have landed on Earth. It's possible that the two planets "regularly exchanged life-forms" over billions of years and "that [humans], in effect, are the Martians." Martian space probes may eventually answer the questions: Is there life on Mars? Did Martian life invade Earth? Are humans the "little green men" of science fiction?

The idea would probably make Carl laugh. "He had a great sense of humor and the wildest, most uninhibited laugh of any person I've ever heard," Annie recalls. His laugh lives on as one of the Earth sounds on the *Voyager* discs. Twenty-two years after it was launched, *Voyager 1* is about 7 billion miles from Earth. It will become the first human-made object to enter interstellar space. Perhaps billions of years from now, in a galaxy billions of light-years away, an alien will hear Carl's laugh, look up at the stars, and wonder.

I know of a world with a million moons. I know of a sun the size of the Earth—made of diamond. . . . The universe is vast and awesome, and for the first time we are becoming a part of it.

—*Carl Sagan*

# SOURCES

1 "Carl Sagan: A Tribute," *Odyssey: Adventures in Science,* April 1998, back cover.

8 Henry Cooper, "Profiles," *New Yorker,* June 28, 1978, 74.

20 Edgar Rice Burroughs, *A Princess of Mars* (New York: Carroll & Graf, 1989), n.p.

21 Cooper, 75.

22 Carl Sagan, "Growing up with Science Fiction," *New York Times,* May 28, 1978, 24.

23 "Sagan, Carl," *Something About the Author* (New York: Gale Research, 1990), 162.

27 Cooper, 75.

38 Ibid., 79.

38 Ibid.

40 "Sagan, Carl," 164.

48 Carl Sagan, *Demon-Haunted World* (New York: Random House, 1995), 49.

53 Carl Sagan, "Mars: A New World to Explore," *National Geographic,* December 1967, 841.

75 Frederic Golden, "The Cosmic Explainer," *Time,* October 20, 1980, 69.

76 Bart Barnes, "Carl Sagan, Who Reached for the Stars and Touched Millions, Dies at 62," *Washington Post,* December 21, 1996, n. p.

80 Judi Kesselman-Turkel, "The Marketing of Dr. Carl Sagan," *Omni,* June 1982, 114.

92 Ann Druyan, telephone interview by the authors, April 5, 1999.

97 "Sagan's Widow and Writing Partner Presses On," *Florida Today,* July 5, 1997, 20.

97 Ibid.

98 Christopher Chyba, "Carl Sagan, Teacher," *The Planetary Report,* May/June 1997, 4.

100 William Broad, "Even in Death, Carl Sagan's Influence Is Still Cosmic," *New York Times,* November 30, 1998, D5.

101   Ibid.
102   William Broad, "Wanna See a Real Live Martian? Try the Mirror," *New York Times*, March 14, 1999, WK 3.
103   "Carl Sagan: A Tribute," 44–45.
103   Carl Sagan, *The Cosmic Connection* (New York: Doubleday, 1973), 51.

# GLOSSARY

**amino acids:** chemical substances that are the basic components of proteins

**astronomy:** the study of heavenly bodies and other matter beyond Earth's atmosphere

**astrophysics:** a branch of astronomy concerned with the physics and chemistry of heavenly bodies and events

**binary code:** a system that uses 0's and 1's to represent letters, numbers, and other characters in a computer

**DNA (deoxyribonucleic acid):** the material that makes up the genes found in nearly all living organisms

**evolution:** a gradual process by which species develop from earlier life-forms

**exobiology (astrobiology):** the study of life outside Earth. It includes the origin of the planets, stars, and galaxies and the chemistry of the universe.

**extraterrestrial:** outside Earth or its atmosphere

**genetics:** the study of the way in which physical characteristics are passed from one generation to another

**greenhouse effect:** the warming of Earth's surface and lower atmosphere that occurs when carbon dioxide and other gases trap the Sun's energy as heat. Greenhouse gases allow light from the Sun to reach Earth's surface and warm it but prevent heat from radiating back into space.

**interstellar:** located or traveling among the stars

**light-year:** the distance light travels in one year, nearly six trillion miles

**proteins:** chemical substances made up of chains of amino acids that are an essential part of all living organisms

**radiation:** energy given off in the form of electromagnetic waves or moving particles

**radio astronomy:** astronomy dealing with radio waves received from outside Earth's atmosphere

**radio telescope:** a large antenna connected to a sensitive receiver that can pick up radio signals from sources outside Earth's atmosphere

**reflector telescope:** a telescope that uses a mirror to produce an image

**refractor telescope:** a telescope that uses a lens to produce an image

**scientific method:** principles and procedures for identifying problems, collecting data, and formulating and testing hypotheses

**X rays:** radiation that has a very short wavelength and is able to pass through opaque objects

# SELECTED BIBLIOGRAPHY

### BOOKS

Sagan, Carl. *Billions and Billions: Thoughts on Life and Death at the Brink of the Millennium.* New York: Random House, 1997.
_____. *Cosmic Connection: An Extraterrestrial Perspective.* Garden City, New York: Anchor Press, 1973.
_____. *Demon-Haunted World: Science as a Candle in the Dark.* New York: Random House, 1995.
_____. *Murmurs of Earth: The Voyager Interstellar Record.* New York: Random House, 1978.
_____. *Pale Blue Dot: A Vision of the Human Future in Space.* New York: Random House, 1994.

### MAGAZINE ARTICLES

Bingham, Roger. "The New Scientist Interview: Carl Sagan." *New Scientist,* January 17, 1980.
Chyba, Christopher. "Carl Sagan, Teacher." *The Planetary Report,* May/June 1997.
Cooper, Henry. "Profiles." *New Yorker,* June 21, 1976.
_____. "Profiles." *New Yorker,* June 28, 1978.
Gelman, David et al. "Seeking Other Worlds." *Newsweek,* August 15, 1977.
Golden, Frederic, and P. Stoler. "The Cosmic Explainer." *Time,* October 20, 1980.
Kesselman-Turkel, Judi, and F. Peterson. "The Marketing of Dr. Carl Sagan." *Omni,* June 1982.
Kluger, Jeffrey. "Uncovering the Secrets of Mars." *Time,* July 14, 1997.
Newcott, William. "Return to Mars." *National Geographic,* August 1998.
Sagan, Carl. "Mars: A New World to Explore." *National Geographic,* December 1967.
"Sagan's Widow and Writing Partner Presses On." *Florida Today,* July 5, 1997.
"A Slayer of Demons." *Psychology Today,* January/February 1996.

Stevenson, Dave, and Diane Ackerman. "Carl Sagan
   Remembered." *Astronomy*, April 1997.
Waters, Harry F. "Public TV's Finest Week." *Newsweek*, October 6,
   1980.

### INTERVIEWS
Ann Druyan, telephone interview by the authors, April 5, 1999.
Cari Sagan Greene, on-line interview by the authors, August 17,
   1998.

### ELECTRONIC MEDIA
Arnett, Bill. "Mars." *Nine Planets*, May 27, 1999.
   <http://seds.lpl.arizona.edu/nineplanets>.
"Carl Sagan, Cornell Astronomer Dies Today (December 20) in
   Seattle." *Cornell News*, December 20, 1996.
   <www.news.cornell.edu>.
"Exploring Mars." *Exploring Mars*, September 19, 1998.
   <www.exploringmars.org>.
Keye, Bradley. "What Is SETI?" *The Active Mind*, April 15, 1996.
   <www.activemind.com>.
"Mars—The Red Planet." *Science Net—Historical Mars Missions*.
   n.d. <www.campus.bt.com/public/ScienceNet>.
McNatt, Glenn. "Reality Is in the Eyes of Beholders." *Sunspot*,
   September 18, 1998. <www.sunspot.net>.

# INDEX

# OTHER TITLES FROM LERNER AND A&E®:

Arthur Ashe
Bill Gates
Bruce Lee
Chief Crazy Horse
Christopher Reeve
Eleanor Roosevelt
George Lucas
Gloria Estefan
Jack London
Jacques Cousteau
Jesse Owens
Jesse Ventura
John Glenn
Legends of Dracula
Legends of Santa Claus

Louisa May Alcott
Madeleine Albright
Maya Angelou
Mohandas Gandhi
Mother Teresa
Nelson Mandela
Princess Diana
Queen Cleopatra
Queen Latifah
Rosie O'Donnell
Saint Joan of Arc
Wilma Rudolph
Women in Space
Women of the Wild West

# ABOUT THE AUTHORS

As a research librarian in public and university libraries, Ellen R. Butts did everything with books but write them. That changed when she and Joyce began writing for a children's science magazine. Ellen and her husband, Al, live in Chevy Chase, Maryland. They have two grown sons.

Joyce R. Schwartz enjoys writing about science and scientists. She began her writing career, with Ellen, as a contributor to a children's science magazine. They then began writing children's books together. Joyce and her husband, Richard, live in Chevy Chase, Maryland. They are the parents of two grown children.